Tenterden Then & Now

Jack Gillett and Peter Webb

YouByYou Books

ISBN 978-0-9564537-9-2

A donation from the sale of this book will be made to Tenterden Day Centre and Tenterden Lions Club.

Typeset in Calibri 9pt

Designed by
Afterhours Artwork, Cranbrook, Kent
Email: *art@afterhours.myzen.co.uk*

Printed by
Berforts, Hastings, East Sussex
www.berforts.co.uk

YouByYou Books,
Swallow Court,
High Halden Road,
Biddenden,
Kent TN27 8BD.
www.youbyyou.co.uk

Contents

Introduction

Tenterden is the Jewel of the Weald and this book endeavours to show that it has been a jewel for many years. When visitors are asked what they like about the town, they usually mention the wide High Street with its green borders, the traditional shops and the mix of building styles. A place that has an old-fashioned charm yet, conversely, is also modern. By comparing old pictures with the same view today, we have shown how Tenterden has changed over the last century yet retained its individuality, so often missing from other places.

The idea for the book came after we had written a few 'Then and Now' articles for the local church parish magazine. Jack has a collection of postcards relating to the old Borough of Tenterden whilst Peter was keen to take the modern equivalent picture and analyse what changes had occurred.

The authors, who first met when they were both on the committee of Tenterden and District National Trust Association, hope readers will be interested in seeing how things have altered.

Jack Gillett and Peter Webb
November 2013

About the Authors

Jack Gillett

Peter Webb

Jack was born in Tenterden, but after going to Nottingham University, spent his working life as a mathematics lecturer in Higher Education. On retiring in 1996 he came back to live in Tenterden and is a member of the local History Society.

Peter was born in Penshurst, Kent, and after National Service had careers with HM Customs and Excise and the International Monetary Fund. After working in many countries, helping them to become less corrupt and more efficient, he retired to Tenterden. He is a keen gardener and, with his wife, judges gardens for the Kent Wildlife Trust.

Acknowledgements

Kentish Express

Kent Messenger

Tenterden – A Pictorial History of a Market Town in the Weald of Kent R.S. Spelling, 1985

Tenterden in Times Past R.S. Spelling, 1991

Tenterden – The First Thousand Years Hugh Roberts, 1995

History of the Churches in the Area during the Second Millennium Tenterden and District Local History Society, 2000

Tenterden in the 20th Century Tenterden and District Local History Society, 2005

Finding Sampson Penley Alan Stockwell, 2012

Tenterden and District Local History Society

HIT Entertainment for Thomas the Tank Engine™

Kent & East Sussex Railway

Tenterden Town Council for the Tenterden Coat of Arms

The owners of the businesses and houses that are featured in this book

Aerial View Looking East From The Church Tower

These views looking east from the top of the church tower show just how much the town has developed. In the old picture, almost everything beyond the High Street is fields. The rooftops in the trees beyond the recreation ground are those of Elmfield, built in the first decade of the last century. The foreground shows the High Street with the ivy-covered Ye Olde Cellars public house and the tall chimneys of Ivy Court House beyond. The Cellars building is now hidden by a tree but the roofline from there to Sayers Lane is little changed. The building on the far right, now occupied by Laura Ashley, was Banisters, the corn merchants. Today, traces can still be seen of the winding gear which was used to hoist

corn to the upper floors. The building is an example of how mathematical tiles, shaped to look like bricks, were used to give the appearance of brick.

The two largest new buildings are the Waitrose supermarket which can be seen on the right hand of the picture and the white roof of what was the Embassy Cinema and is now the fashion shop, M&Co. Beyond the big blue recycling bin behind this building, the recreation ground can just be glimpsed and in front of the bin is the edge of the new Market Square, the latest High Street development. Looking further afield there are the roof tops of Shrubcote and other housing that has been built along the Appledore Road.

Ivy Court

These two pictures probably show one of the most dramatic changes in the High Street. Ivy Court House was a grand house that had a commanding position with a large garden at the eastern end of the High Street. Its roof is still clearly visible above the fronts of Café Nero and Phase Eight and its original doorway, one of the most handsome features, was brought forward to the building line, the shops – built around the 1930s – sadly obliterating the wide front garden which

made it a splendidly traditional and 'green' part of the High Street. It is likely that the gardens at the rear of the house would have extended to the present Waitrose car park and may have included what is now Ivy Court Surgery. Recreation Ground Road runs to the left of the wooden gates that can be seen in the old photograph. This was published as a postcard by S. Beeken of Tenterden but they got the name of the house wrong and called it 'East Court'.

The land between Ivy Court and what was then Ye Olde Cellars Public House was sold and the Embassy Cinema which opened in February 1937, just after the closure of the Picture Theatre in Oaks Road, was built on it. The cinema closed in 1969 and became various supermarkets before the present fashion store M&Co took the premises.

TENTERDEN CRICKET

1901 team v. Great Chart at Morghew Park, 17 August: back row (l to r): G. Hilder, F. Pellatt, unknown, C. De Foe Baker, unknown, T.E. Rammell
seated (l to r): Dr R A Skinner, A E Bishop, W H Dixon, G H Baker front (l to r): unknown. A. Wenham
The unknown players are A.L. Poile, A.E. Baker and H.E. Scoones. It hasn't been possible to match the names to the faces.

The earliest known record of cricket in Tenterden is in the *Kentish Post* on 20 August 1755 when it announced a game between the Gentlemen of Tenterden in Kent and the Gentlemen of Mayfield in Sussex 'for a crown a man... and with a good ordinary at the White Lion.' Although some details of early matches are known, the first reference to a Cricket Club in Tenterden was in the *Maidstone Gazette* on 11 August 1840.

Cricket Week was established in 1880 when the Tenterden Cricket Club was playing in one of the 'Six Fields' that lie between the town and the Smallhythe Road. It continued until the First World War and was resurrected in 1959 since when it has taken place every year.

Tenterden v Mayor of Tenterden XI, Tenterden Cricket Festival – Friday 4 August 2000:
back row (l to r): J. Wilson (umpire), J. Saunders, T. Russell, T. Piper, R. Turney, B. Peachey, J. Curteis, J.R. Gillett (scorer), S. Saha, J. Parkman Snr, S. Smith, S. Kirk, K. Makin, L. Bates, D. Paine, J. Marsh, J. Williams, G. Pickford (umpire), D. Knight
front (l to r): D. McDonald, M. Bridge, M. Upton (Tenterden captain), Cllr. Mrs J. Kirk (Mayor of Tenterden), M. French (Mayor's Captain), M. Pearman, D. Dales

In 1887 a political dispute caused an 'eruption' that brought an end to the original club and another, Tenterden Park Cricket Club, was formed. It started playing a short distance away in the picturesque Morghew Park (which the club owns) on the other side of the Smallhythe Road. This was the forerunner of the present club, the word Park being dropped after the First World War. Between the Wars, the club played on Saturdays and also ran a Wednesday Eleven. Sunday cricket became popular after the Second World War.

The present pavilion, seen in the modern picture, has been refurbished and extended several times since it opened in 1970. It replaced an old wooden building. The opening of the pavilion was marked with a match against a Kent XI, captained by Colin Cowdrey, on 13 May 1970. In April 1992 the Club bought the freehold of the three and three-quarter acre ground from owner John Leroy for £20,000.

Between 1977 and 1994 Tenterden played in the East Sussex League. In 1995, the Club joined the East Kent League and then the Kent League in 1996 for Saturday cricket. Over the past few years many players have graduated from the successful colts sides. Today there is a Sunday team and additionally there is cricket at Tenterden most Wednesdays from May to October.

The Old Manor House, High Street

The 17th century manor house in Tenterden High Street was well known for its magnificent rose hedge and long brick path. For 100 years it was the home of the Thomson family who published the renowned Thomson's Almanac and Directory from a building at the side. There was always a box by the gate for donations to Princess Alexandra's Rose Day charity.

When the house eventually came on the market, many people thought it should be kept as part of Tenterden's heritage but nobody had the money either to buy it or carry out the repairs to eradicate woodworm and dry rot. The cost was

estimated at £8,000 – a small fortune at the time. Kent County Council refused planning permission for the business development of the land but, because it was a prime site in the middle of the High Street, the Minister of Housing and local Government in Whitehall reversed the Council's decision. At an auction in the Town Hall, the property was sold for £5,000.

The house was demolished in 1955 and the site cleared, but it was derelict until the Manor Row terrace of shops and flats was completed early in the 1960s, after years of debate over the development. When you look at Manor Row today with its coffee shop, furniture store and The Gateway, which houses the Post Office, it is very difficult to envisage a rather grand manor house with a beautiful rose hedge and lawns.

Boormans

Boormans, which stood at the west end of Tenterden High Street, was regarded by some as the 'Harrods of the Weald'. The company's motto was 'Value for Money' and it sold everything from a bag of sugar to a hat; ran a horse-drawn funeral service and could completely furnish your home. Founded in 1819 by Samuel Boorman, the firm rapidly prospered and expanded under his son Henry's control. H. Boorman and Co. had branches in Headcorn, Benenden, Smarden, Appledore, Wittersham, Bethersden, Iden Green and Rolvenden. They employed 40 people, some of whom lived on the

premises. The business survived for 153 years before closing in February 1973. In the last week shoppers were able to buy groceries at a discount of 10 per cent! At the time of its closure, all the branches had closed and the firm had reduced to 20 employees as the focus of commercial activity in Tenterden shifted to the other end of town and people had also become more mobile and could travel further afield to shop.

Most of the 18th century buildings were demolished about 1977 with the exception of what is now the Orvis Store. They were replaced with flats known as Caxton Close.

The William Caxton Inn (formerly the Black Horse inn)

This early 20th century scene with its horse-drawn snowplough was taken at a corner of the town that has changed remarkably little in 100 years. The pub, then The Black Horse, is a typical Wealden inn and was probably a well-known resort for smugglers. When Messrs O. Edwards and Son ran a brewery behind The Vine Public House in Tenterden, they supplied The Black Horse, along with The New Inn (now Honeymoon Chinese Restaurant at 3 East Cross), with beer.

During the 1951 Festival of Britain celebrations, there was an exhibition in the Town Hall which included books from the time of Caxton – the first man to set up a printing press in England and reputedly born in the town around 1422. It showed the history of printing and well-known authors gave talks. The pub was renamed in his honour when the Mayor of Tenterden, Cllr. A.J. Wright, unveiled a new sign. This colourful sign, which was featured in Whitbread's series of inn signs, was based on a woodcut of King Canute learning chess, from 'The Philosopher' in 'The Game and Playe of the Chesse' (1474), one of Caxton's most famous productions. The pub is now owned by Shepherd Neame and the sign shows a man using an old printing press.

The modern photograph taken from the same spot shows an almost identical roof line but the large yew tree by the side of the pub has gone. The internet tells us that a horse-drawn snowplough was still in use in Tenterden during the big freeze of 1938. Men sat on the back of the snowplough to weigh it down and children loved to take part – probably just as efficient as the modern lorry and a lot more fun and interest.

NATIONAL SCHOOL, CHURCH ROAD

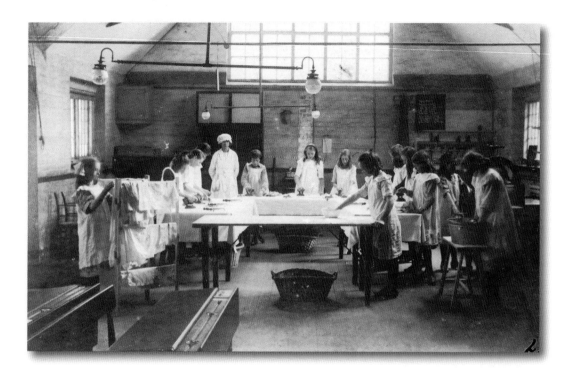

This was the plight that faced girls when they joined the senior school in the 1920s. The picture shows girls at the National School which was opened in 1843 and occupies the site of the present Day Centre in Church Road. Some may think subjects such as Maths are tedious today, but imagine being taught how to wash, scrub and iron laundry.

The Tenterden National School was established in Church Road, formerly School Lane, in 1843, and the date is still visible on the building. In 1957 the British School, in Ashford Road, closed and at the same time the National School moved its

8-11 year-olds to a new Junior School in Recreation Ground Road leaving the National School as an Infants school. In 1973 the 150 pupils of the Infant School also moved to new purpose-built premises in Recreation Ground Road adjacent to the Junior School and the school buildings in Church Road became the Tenterden Day Centre.

The Tenterden Day Centre provides a place where the elderly and lonely can socialise and get a coffee and a meal. Tenterden Disabled In Action and Helping Hands are also in the building. The Day Centre is used by up to 25 people every day with over 120 members. The Disabled Unit cares for 50 members and Helping Hands provides over 200 hours of support. None of this would be possible without the many volunteers who also help with outings and holidays for the elderly and disabled.

HOMEWOOD HOUSE

Funeral of the late Mayor of Tenterden, Admiral Sir Chas Drury. May 23rd 1914.

Homewood House, now Homewood School, on the Ashford Road, was built by James Haffenden in 1766 in the fashionable neo-classical style. Its most celebrated (although short-lived) resident was Admiral Sir Charles Drury (pictured) who bought it in 1910 and settled there on his retirement, building several additions to the house. Charles Carter Drury was born in New Brunswick, Canada, in 1846, joined the Royal Navy in 1859 and held many important commands around the world before becoming an Admiral in 1908. He became a member of the Tenterden Borough Council on 1 November 1913 and a week later was chosen as Mayor. He died from an apoplectic seizure on 18 May

1914 and was buried in Tenterden Cemetery. In an effort to provide peace and quiet during his illness, a long section of the Ashford Road outside Homewood House was heavily sanded to deaden the noise of horses' hooves. Lady Drury continued to live at Homewood and the grounds were used for fêtes, pageants, etc., and the Women's Institute met there regularly.

During the Second World War, Homewood was taken over by the military. In June 1947, Lady Drury sold Homewood to Kent County Council Education Committee. She was fond of children and wanted the house to be used as a school rather than a hotel or nursing home as had been proposed. Alderman Mrs E.A. Adams, the first lady mayor of Tenterden (1937-1939) and the prime mover for a Central School in the town before the War, together with other local residents, supported her and she sold the house with its 50 acres for £10,000. With numerous additions, extensions and adaptations (the wartime wooden huts erected by the Army were used as classrooms), Homewood School opened partially in 1948 and fully in April 1949 with pupils of secondary age transferring from the schools around. Mrs Adams became the first Chairman of Governors. Homewood School and Sixth Form Centre is now a Foundation School with specialist status for Performing Arts and Vocational Education. It is one of the largest schools in Kent with more than 2,100 students, of whom 400 or so are in the Sixth Form.

The view of the back of the house is also little altered although a fire escape has been added. But where there were once extensive gardens with a croquet lawn and a tennis court, there are now several purpose-built classrooms, the Sinden Theatre, a new library and sports hall. The small lawn that remains is used by boys and girls in their smart new uniforms rather than fashionable ladies wearing large floral hats.

OLD CINEMA, THE FAIRINGS

TENTERDEN. PICTURE THEATRE

The cinema, built in 1912 and originally called the Picture Theatre, was regarded as one of the finest and best equipped in the South of England. Subsequently, because it was lit by electricity throughout, it was renamed the Electric Palace. Programmes were changed on Mondays and Thursdays and it was open every evening, except for Sundays, and on Saturday afternoons. Locally, it became known affectionately as the 'Picture Palace' and seat prices were 5d, 9d and 1s 3d (old money) with a special half price for children at matinees. It was closed in February 1937 and was replaced by the larger Embassy Cinema in the High Street.

During the Second World War the building was used as an Army Supply Depot and in the 1950s was nearly pulled down but was redeveloped into shops, unusually built into the side of the cinema, and offices. At the Ashford Road end of the building are some steps to a sandwich bar and this may have originally been the projectionist's entrance.

Until recently one could see the words 'Picture Theatre' on the large semi-circular plaster above the office of Hobbs Parker but the words have now disappeared. The attractive roof tiles have also disappeared and the upper storey of the estate agent's office has replaced the half dome over the entrance.

The cinema was built on ground formerly occupied by Oaks House, a half-timbered house that had grounds extending to all the space between Oaks Road and Ashford Road. It was pulled down in 1830 and in 1836 six houses (now 1 - 6 Oaks Place) were built on part of the site.

LEIGH GREEN WINDMILL

Leigh Green near Tenterden.

Leigh Green Mill on the Appledore Road was the last of the borough's windmills until it burned down in a spectacular blaze on 26 November 1913. *The Kentish Express* reported: "The windmill and stores were burned out, much damage being done to valuable machinery and to a large stock of oilcake, etc. Some portion of the stock of corn was saved and the bake houses, not being attached to the mill, escaped damage. The conflagration presented a grand sight, being

situated in an open position, and could be seen for many miles." At the time the mill belonged to a Mrs Pilbeam and was let to Messrs. Foster and Ward. It had been built in 1819 and was started by Mr Edward Killick, whose name and the date appeared on one of the old oak beams. The roadside cottages behind which it stood are still there.

SMALLHYTHE PLACE
THE FORMER HOME OF VICTORIAN ACTRESS DAME ELLEN TERRY

'MISS ELLEN TERRY'S COTTAGE'

Smallhythe Place was built in the first half of the 16th century, perhaps following the great fire of 1514 which destroyed most of Smallhythe. In the late 1890s, during their unrivalled stage partnership, Ellen Terry (photographed above, aged 16, by Julia Margaret Cameron), renowned both as the finest Shakespearean actress of her day and for her colourful personal life, was driving along the lane with Sir Henry Irving, the great actor. She is said to have spotted this old farmhouse, with dark timbers, a sloping tiled roof and large chimney stack and immediately declared that it was the place she would like to live and die. Ellen bought the property when it came on the market in 1899 and lived there until her death on 21 July 1928, aged 81.

Her admirers and friends included the greatest painters, poets, politicians and writers of the day and her career ran from child roles in touring productions, to triumph on the London stage, US tours and a series of film roles. Her daughter Edith Craig spent much of the rest of her life making Smallhythe Place a shrine to Ellen. In 1938 the National Trust agreed to take on the property subject to Edith retaining a life-interest. Edith died in 1947. The property also has a barn which, it had been suggested to Ellen, should be a theatre. In 1931, Edith took up the idea and established the Barn Theatre Society, running it on a subscription basis in much the same way as it remains today.

Smallhythe Place is now a favourite venue for members of the National Trust and for overseas visitors. Between 40,000 and 60,000 people visit each year. Much of the interior of the house is how it was in Ellen Terry's time and rooms are used to display the magnificent dresses and cloaks that she wore on stage. Open air theatre and plays and music in the Barn Theatre are also attractions. The garden is much as it was but the reeds round the small pond have grown and boating is no longer an option.

QUOITS

TENTERDEN QUOIT CLUB

This early 20th century picture shows Tenterden Quoits Club standing on the greens outside its headquarters, the New Inn at East Cross. Quoits involved throwing a flat iron ring at a mark and required a strong arm. The Club Secretary was George Rummery, the New Inn landlord. Standing in the back row with a straw hat and bow tie is George Warwick, father of Neil Warwick. Between them they ran a shop at 27 High Street for 79 years, selling tobacco, confectionery, sports goods, etc.

The New Inn, originally owned by Edwards Brewery, was acquired by Whitbreads and around 1950 was renamed the Ancient Borough, with its sign depicting the Tenterden Coat of Arms. A few years later it closed down and became the Loong Sing Chinese Restaurant, now the Honeymoon.

Quoits may no longer be played in Tenterden but there are plenty of new ways to keep fit in the recreation ground opposite the site of the original picture.

BISHOP'S STONEMASONS

OLD TENTERDEN. BISHOP'S STONEMASONS YARD.

Where the brick houses Nos. 71 and 73 High Street stand today, stood this early timber-framed building of the 15th or 16th century. One can just see the wall and tall chimney of the Zion Baptist Church which was next door. The dormer windows were installed in the 17th century and below the large one was a passageway for carts to pass through. During the 19th century the Bishop family lived in it and had their stonemason business in the front yard. It was run by

Mr George Bishop and when he died in 1844 the business continued under his widow, Mary, and son Stephen, together with Mr Henry Pennells, a bricklayer. A few years later Mr Pennells became a stonemason and took over the business in 1858. The old house was pulled down in 1874. Mr Pennells died in 1880, whilst Stephen Bishop lived until 1899.

There is absolutely no sign of the stonemason's house or business today. Using the wall of the Zion Baptist Church as a guide you can see that the houses that now occupy the site were built in what had been the stonemason's yard. Residences have replaced a busy business. Neat front gardens, an inviting seat and a convenient bus stop and litter bin together with trees give shade where none existed before. One wonders how many unfinished gravestones are under the foundations of the houses!

THE RELIANCE BUS OUTSIDE THE WOOLPACK

The Reliance bus service seen here outside the 16th century Woolpack Hotel was started in February 1912 by the Sutton Valence Motor Bus Company, owned by Ernest Neve of Chart Sutton. *The Kent Messenger* reported: "Mr Neve has secured one of the latest motor buses which ensures service de luxe." It started with two trips a day from Tenterden to Maidstone. Reliance was bought out by the Maidstone and District Bus Company in 1916.

The bus stop now is outside the adjacent Town Hall. The Woolpack has lost its ivy but recently acquired a splendid new coloured sign on a metal bracket and some outdoor tables. The hand-written blackboard advertises a 'Pig and Ale Fest'. A decorative direction sign surmounted with the town's crest has replaced the tree outside the Town Hall.

SMALLHYTHE PORT

Smallhythe was originally the port for Tenterden with an important ship building industry in the 14th and 15th centuries. Warships were built using timber from the nearby Wealden Forest and in 1538 the port was visited by King Henry VIII to see his newest warship *The Grand Masters* being built. Cargoes of wool and other goods were shipped to the continent.

Storms caused the Rother to change its course and with silting the port lost its importance. However boats, as the picture shows, were still able to navigate from the Rother along the Reading Sewer as far as Smallhythe until the early years of the last century. Behind the boat is the Toll Gate House and to the right of the tree is Smallhythe Place, thought to have been either the Harbour Master's house or the Customs House. It eventually became the home of the Victorian actress, Ellen Terry. Today, it is difficult to imagine boats on this stretch of water as it has shrunk to little more than an overgrown stream.

St. Michaels School and Church

St. Michaels, Tenterden, Church and School

The school was opened in 1862 on land bought by Mr Seaman Beale, who lived at Finchden Manor, Tenterden. His son, one of the Tenterden curates, Rev. Seaman Curteis Tress Beale, had been taking regular Sunday services in the wheelwright's shop which stood at the east end of the area known as the Pavement. When the school was built the congregation from the local population of around 600 moved there.

Mr Beale senior then turned his attention to building a church. Although funds were raised locally, he made a large contribution to the £9,000 that the land and building cost. Until the church was built, the hamlet was known as Bore's Isle or Bird's Isle and it thus became the village of St. Michael's (the apostrophe is now usually dropped). Rev. Beale became the first vicar of St. Michaels (1863-1881) and died aged 53 in 1885. The church spire was added in 1875 and a clock installed in 1884.

The church was consecrated on Saturday 1 August 1863 by Dr. Longley, the Archbishop of Canterbury, and dedicated to St. Michael and All Angels. The building had commenced 12 months previously with Mrs E.J. Eyres (née Parker and from 1865 the wife of Admiral Gordon of Ingleden), the widow of Capt H. Eyres CB, laying the foundation stone. In 1993 the silver trowel that she used was rediscovered in Wilby, Suffolk. It was in the hands of Ann Marriott, a great-great niece of Admiral Gordon. It carries the inscription: *To the glory of God the foundation stone of St. Michael's Church Tenterden was laid on the 31st day of July 1862*. Mr Bourne of Woodchurch built the church of Kentish ragstone and Bath stone with Mr Gordon M. Hills of London as the architect.

The school has lost its bell tower, but a chimney has been added and there are some flat-roofed extension classrooms. A cockerel has been added to the top of the church spire.

EASTGATE

Eastgate House, formerly known as Prospect House, was built in 1741. It stood along the Woodchurch Road in 6.75 acres of land. In 1919 it was owned by Seaman Beale who sold it to the distinguished retired judge Sir James Mellor, a former Senior Master of the Supreme Court, King's Remembrancer, King's Coroner and Registrar of the Court of Criminal Appeal.

When Sir James died in 1926 it was bought by Dr. and Mrs Martin. Dr. Martin, born in Cornwall and educated at Sherborne and St. Bartholomew's Hospital, London, had practised at Reading, Berkshire, for 26 years. He was elected to the Borough Council in 1929, served as Mayor in 1932 and 1933 and was made an Alderman in November 1938.

By the 1960s the house had fallen into disrepair and despite public pressure to keep it, the property was demolished in 1964. In its place, 30 new Georgian style houses were built to make today's Mount Pleasant, Martins Close and Eastgate Road. The only visible connection with the past is the boundary wall along the main road.

Tenterden Brewery

Felling the Chimney, Tenterden Brewery
July 1922.

Our old picture shows the toppling of the chimney after Tenterden Brewery closed in the early 1920s. It had been set up at the end of the 18th century by Isaac Cloake at what is today the rear of the Vine Inn. After Cloake's death, the brewery passed to Samuel Shepherd. Mr Obadiah Edwards purchased the brewery in 1872 and ran it until his death in 1905 when it was carried on by his three sons. As well as the brewery, the Edwards family owned nine pubs in and around Tenterden.

There is nothing to indicate where the brewery once stood and the site is now a coach park. Passengers on two coaches from Belgium are about to disembark to enjoy a day in Tenterden, the town attracts day-trippers from France, Belgium and the Netherlands thanks to Dover's ferries and the Channel Tunnel. The prominent post in the foreground houses a closed circuit television camera, one of several around the town.

RENAUX IN FULL FLIGHT NEAR READING STREET, TENTERDEN, KENT.

This aeroplane flown by an intrepid Frenchman, Renaux, caused a sensation when it was forced to land at Warehorne near the church in 1911. Here it is seen flying over Reading Street, about three miles or so out of Tenterden.

It was taking part in one of the earliest and most ambitious air races, The European Air Race (Paris-Liege-Utrecht-Brussels-Roubaix-Calais-London-Calais-Paris) of 1911. The fleet of monoplanes and biplanes touched down at Whitfield

near Dover before following a series of large arrows made of linen, 100ft long and 10ft wide, which pointed them in the right direction as they made their way to Hendon via Shoreham and on the return trip to Dover.

The detailed account in *The Kentish Express* lyrically sums up the thrill of the race in a report headlined 'Remarkable Flights from Calais'. It reads: "The seventh stage of the Circuit of Europe Air Race organised by *The Standard* and the *Paris Journal* saw a wonderful phase in the history of aviation when eleven airmen flew across the English Channel like a flight of swallows." Renaux's biplane had trouble with its carburettor, which forced him to land at Warehorne, after following the Royal Military Canal. In a very quick space of time, hundreds of spectators flocked to the scene.

Taking a photograph today from the same spot as the 1911 postcard was difficult and involved balancing on the top of a wire fence and being eyed with suspicion by a cow with a calf. Extensive farm buildings have been erected in the meantime and the oast houses in the old picture are completely hidden except for a cowl. Twin silos dominate the horizon.

By Road to Tenterden from the Bull Inn, Rolvenden

This photograph from the early 1900s shows a coach piled high, standing outside the Bull at Rolvenden. The pub was a stopping off place for this two-horse Hook's coach on its route between Ashford, Tenterden and Cranbrook. In the doorway is the licensee at the time Tom Cheeseman, with his niece May Bishop by his side. The coach man was Mr Gilbert and his passengers are Lucy Bishop, May's sister, and Drusilla Cheeseman their cousin. The man in front of the horses is Alfred Judge. May and Lucy were the daughters of the well known local sportsman A.E. 'Bert' Bishop who, like his father Edward Bishop before him, was 'mine host' at the Woolpack Hotel in Tenterden.

The coach then was invariably loaded with all kinds of belongings, including hens and livestock bound for market. The Bull remains a popular inn and has been spruced up with outdoor tables and neat white paling. Jack Gillett, *Tenterden Then and Now* co-author, and descendant of the Bishops, stands in the doorway. There is still a bus stop opposite for services to Cranbrook and Tenterden.

Eastwell House

High Street c. 1900, showing Eastwell House on the right

Eastwell House that stood where Eastwell Parade is now, had a rather grand frontage for a shop. It formerly belonged to the Curteis family. The ground floor was converted into two shops in the early part of the 19th century and these were run by Hugh Willsher Senior who had a greengrocer's shop on the right of the front door and his brother-in-law, Harry Judge, an auctioneer, who had an office on the left. After the death of Hugh Willsher, his sons continued to run the greengrocer's together with a nursery complete with greenhouses on a large area of land at the rear. During the demolition of the house in 1963, workmen found a floral design mural which dated back to Tudor times. The busy modern shops with flats above are not so imposing.

HERONDEN GATEWAY

Tenterden. Herondon Gateway.

The Gateway at the west end of the town is the entrance to Heronden Hall, a 19th century building which replaced an earlier building on the same site. At one time the Hall was the home of the Dampier Palmer family, who were benefactors to the town. At various times the Gateway had been lived in but during the hurricane of October 1987 it was very badly damaged. It remained in a damaged state until the summer of 2009 when the current owners, the

Gledhill Family, started restoring it to its former neo-Gothic Victorian splendour, a task completed in the summer of 2010. All the ivy has gone from the building which now stands beside a very busy road junction.

The Town Hall was built in 1792 and replaced the original Court Hall which was destroyed by fire in 1661 when a man confined to the Court Hall prison for debt burnt the place to the ground. Many historic and valuable documents were destroyed. The upstairs Assembly Room was used as a Magistrate's Court until comparatively recently.

Although the basic building is the same as in our Edwardian photograph, the Town Hall is now much more attractive with its hanging baskets and flags and the paving outside relaid with York stone. The balcony, which was added in 1912, has the town arms on a shield, and as the hall is registered to conduct weddings, is often crowded with wedding guests. Within the hall are eight oil paintings of previous Mayors and High Sheriffs.

Tenterden Town Council was formed following the 1974 reorganisation of local government when the town was absorbed into Ashford Borough.

FIRE STATION

The fire station shown here was originally built in 1823 as the Market Hall. The sign on the side of the Vine pointing to the railway station dates the picture as post-1903, when the railway reached Tenterden. Station Road was much narrower then.

The first fire station for a manual pump was simply a shed built at a cost of £10 in 1848 at the back of the Market House. The shed was later used by the firemen as an office. The picture shows a later pump clearly marked 'Borough of Tenterden', drawn by magnificently groomed horses and manned by firemen with large shiny helmets.

A proposal in 1935 to demolish the fire station and widen Station Road, caused such a storm that the plans were axed. Eventually, it came down after Tenterden Borough Council purchased the site for a nominal £5 in 1972, partly because it was too small for modern fire engines and partly to improve access for the new car parks in Station Road. It was replaced by the current fire station in St. Michaels at a cost of £17,000.

The Vine and the shops beyond have undergone detailed changes and the corner now looks cluttered with a red telephone box, a rubbish bin, a tourist sign post and a CCTV camera at the top of a long pole.

East Cross

This rustic scene from the Edwardian era has given way to what is probably the busiest junction in the town. On the left of the picture is the double-fronted shop of Freddie Allen's grocery store, and next door the New Inn, with the name of O. Edwards & Son, the brewers, above. The grocer's is now a gentlemen's outfitters and the pub a Chinese restaurant.

The hedged triangular garden between Ashford Road and Oaks Road was in private hands until the Council acquired the land after the Second World War. It is now East Cross Gardens and fronts the Fairings. There is a plinth commemorating

the development of the site in 1948 with paving, seats and planting with funds raised by the Women's Voluntary Service, the Chamber of Trade and the Rotary Club and another celebrating the Millennium with a time capsule buried beneath it. If the capsule were to be opened in the year 3000, it would be very interesting to see the changes!

The junction has undergone many changes: with the development of the Waitrose complex in the late 1980s and the increasing traffic in Recreation Ground Road, traffic lights were erected. However, the metal fencing around the recreation ground is still just visible under the trees.

JENNERS, 21-23 ASHFORD ROAD

"Westcliff". Tenterden.

This building in Ashford Road has a long and varied history. When the picture was taken in the early part of the 20th century it was probably used as the Westcliff Boarding House. Later, after the Second World War, part of the building

became Westcliff School, a private school for boys and girls, run by the Wellard family while the other half housed the Linton Café. The Jenner family started their electrical appliance business at No. 23 when the school closed in 1957 and acquired No. 21 on the closure of the café in 1974.

The upper two floors are much the same and on the ground floor the original doors with their decorative windows are still there. The wooden building on the left has been replaced by the Post Office sorting office.

The Grange, St. Michaels

The Grange, St Michaels, near Tenterden

The Grange was the original home of the Diggle family who had a long association with the public life of Tenterden. Formerly Bird's Isle House, it was rebuilt and renamed by Joseph Robert Diggle at the end of the 19th century. He was Mayor of Tenterden on five occasions, 1895, 1896, 1897, 1901 and 1902. When he was first chosen he wasn't even a member of the council, joining that body at the end of his third year of office in 1898. He was born at Pendleton,

Lancashire on 12 May 1849 and educated at Manchester Grammar School and Wadham College, Oxford. He married Jane Wilkinson, daughter of J.W. Macrae of Liverpool and had two sons and two daughters. He entered the Church in 1874, serving as a curate at St Mary's, Bryanston Square, London, but he resigned in 1879 to enter public life and left the ministry a few years later. He became a member of the London School Board, serving from 1879 to 1897 and as Chairman from 1885 to 1894.

Joseph Diggle left Tenterden in 1909 and died at Oxford on 16 January 1917, aged 67. His brother, the Bishop of Carlisle, officiated at the funeral which was held at St. Michaels. The Grange and its contents were sold. His wife died on 11 January 1927, aged 77. Both are buried in St. Michaels Churchyard. His son, Joseph Macrae Diggle, was Mayor of Tenterden in 1923, 1924 and 1936 and played an active part in the town. Another son, W. Wrigley Diggle, was the architect for Tenterden War Memorial.

Between 1917 and 1930 The Grange became Asheton Modern School, a boarding school for boys aged 6 to 18 with H.F. Varley as headmaster. Pupils wore distinctive scarlet blazers. Afterwards it became a rehabilitation centre for jobless men, followed by a home for children with learning difficulties. A German bomb damaged it so severely in 1940 that it was pulled down. New dwellings have taken its place. The picture below shows the junction of Grange Road and Shoreham Lane.

TENTERDEN FOOTBALL

Above: Ye Old Crocks, 27 March 1912; and right: Tenterden Football Club, 1907-8

Main picture: standing l to r: A. Wenham (Treasurer), W.B. MacGowan (Referee), G.L. Turner, F. Burden, H. Amies, A. Apps, W.L. Boyt, E. Fuggle, G. Reeves, G.W. Dapson, G.F. Varty (Hon Secretary), Dr R.A. Skinner (President); seated l to r: A.W. Milne, A. Green, A.W. Pulley (Captain), C. Bates, W. Clapp; front l to r: W Beach, J Clark

Inset, Ye Olde Crocks team, 1912: standing l to r: unknown, unknown, A. Wenham, G. Reeves, A.W. Pulley, unknown, P. Watson, C. Field; seated l to r: B. Bates, A.E. Bishop, W.T. Bark, unknown, ? Thomson

Tenterden Football Club was formed sometime in the 1890s but It was some years before the club played in competitions. In 1904 they entered the Weald of Kent League and four years later the team in this old photograph were victorious. After the Second World War they became very successful and in 1955 the 1st and 2nd XIs won eight trophies between them. In 1973 the 1st XI won the Weald of Kent Charity Shield, Hawkhurst and Ashford Charity Cups and were East Sussex League Champions. In 1982 the Club joined with St. Michaels and became known as Tenterden and St. Michaels United, fielding four senior sides on a Saturday and two junior sides on a Sunday. In 1990 they again won the East Sussex League and other cups including the inaugural Jack Freeman Memorial Trophy. The Club originally played on the recreation ground but in 1966 moved to the adjacent Glebe field where they still play today.

One of the highlights of the football season over many years in Tenterden has been the Weald of Kent Charity Trophy Final for a shield presented by Sir Thomas R. Dewar in 1909. With a few exceptions the final has always been played at Tenterden on Good Friday afternoon. Until the mid-1960s the final attracted large crowds and was a great spectacle for a junior competition, the local equivalent to Wembley, perhaps.

In 1996 the Tenterden Tigers Junior Football Club was formed, providing training sessions and competitive football for children between the ages of 5 and 17. In 2000 the Club launched Project Homeground with the object of acquiring their own pitch, receiving positive support from The Football Association, The Kent County Football Association, Sport England, Tenterden Town Council, Ashford Borough Council and Kent County Council. They have yet to find a home of their own and practice and play on both the Glebe field and recreation ground. The modern photograph shows some very young Tigers training on the Glebe field with professionals from Chelsea Football Club under their Foundation Scheme.

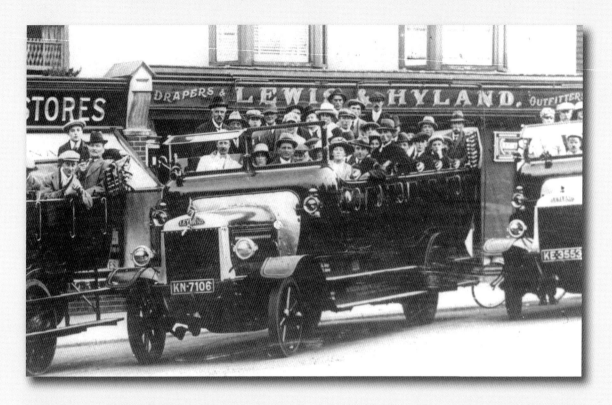

It was not unusual in the 1920s for businesses, firms, shops and clubs to organise day trips for their staff or members. This Leyland charabanc was one of three leaving from the International Stores at 72 High Street (now Vision Express, the opticians). Dymchurch was one popular destination. Note that everyone, both male and female, is wearing a hat, although the vehicle has a folding roof at the rear. The man sitting by the front door appears to have a musical instrument which he would use to help the singsong on the way home!

The stop is now used by regular bus services to Ashford, Maidstone, Tunbridge Wells and Rye. The bus shown in the modern picture is the Renown Company's service to Tunbridge Wells. Excursion coaches, of which there are still plenty to and from the town, use the Station Road car park.

Kent Old Grammar School, Tenterden.

One of the oldest buildings in the town, Nos. 18 and 20 High Street, served as the Tenterden Grammar School for more than 300 years. Its use as such was recorded in 1521 but it is thought to date from the previous century. When the school closed in 1812 there were only six pupils and its endowments were transferred to the National Society which eventually built a new National School in Church Road in 1843.

In the early 1900s, a Mr Hatcher used part of the building as a small florist shop before Mr Charlie Hyland took it over selling fruit and vegetables as well as flowers. In the late 1950s, Mr R.M. Weeks renovated the building and opened an impressive men's outfitters shop. The building retained its fine roof, which is supported by a splendid crown post, but gained a dormer window and lost a chimney. The shop has changed hands a number of times in recent years and now trades as Country Casuals and Viyella. Just inside the shop is the shield commemorating its use as a school and its restoration. At the back, on one of the roof beams there is a list of some of the drapery items once sold.

Police Station and Temperance Hotel

The old police station was built on the site of a wooden toll house which was taken down around 1880. If you peep through the window of what is now a ladies' hairdressers you can still see the bars of the old cell. It remained the police station until 1956 when a new one was built in Oaks Road, although that has also now closed. The Tenterden Borough Police Force which consisted of a High Constable and three Constables survived until the Local Government Act of 1888 abolished police forces run by Boroughs with a population of less than 10,000.

When the Police Station closed it was taken over by Rye Model Laundry, followed by a music shop called Jailhouse Rock, and then the hairdresser. Cassingham's Temperance Hotel on the opposite corner is now a ladies fashion shop and a Prezzo restaurant.

The Old Horse Pond, St. Michaels

St. Michael's.   Near Tenterden

The old horse pond along Grange Road is now partly beneath the site of the present village hall and partly under the garages at the entrance to Marshalls Land. It afforded a wonderful view of the church and school before the village hall was built in 1967. The housing development took place in the early 1950s and was named after the farm a little further up Grange Road on whose land it was built.

ASHFORD ROAD, TENTERDEN

You would have a hard time driving sheep along the Ashford Road these days! The large square house on the right, just before what is now Turners Avenue, is Clifton House. Built in 1873, it became an emergency hospital in 1914 run by Voluntary Aid Detachment (VAD) nurses. Wounded servicemen from Belgium, Canada, Australia and Britain were treated there on beds and furniture lent by local residents. When the first 15 Belgian soldiers arrived on 30 November 1914 all the beds were ready and hot food available. Its full complement of around 20 beds was nearly always occupied. Dr. W.E. Dring was the doctor in charge and his senior staff included Miss Cicely Peel (of Heronden) and Miss V. Milne (of The Croft, Elmfield). The Tenterden townspeople were generous with their gifts of fruit, vegetables and cakes and funds to supplement the Government grant to Clifton House.

The shops at 35, 37, 39 and 41 High Street stand where the road narrows. All have changed hands and trades except for No. 37 which has been a baker's since 1895 when it was taken over by the Goldsmith family who ran it until they sold it in 1975. It is now Avards, the Village Bakery. No. 35, Allens, the Fishmongers and Poulterers, is now East ladies fashion,

Marchants (which until 1905 was Lloyds Bank) is now Mostyn McKenzie shoes and Winser the grocers is the Nationwide Building Society. To the right at No. 43 is the former Eight Bells public house, once known as 'The Angel' and then 'Six Bells' and then Eight. It is now the Café Rouge restaurant.

FINCHDEN MANOR

The Priory, Tenterden

St. Benedict's Cottages, Tenterden

Finchden is situated just over a mile from Tenterden on the Appledore Road. In medieval times it was the home of the Finch Family from whom it got its name. At its core is a 15th century house with additions and alterations from the 16th and early 17th centuries. In the 19th century there were major additions, including a neo-Gothic Great Hall built by Lady Chatterton, who purchased the house in 1860. The farm opposite bears the name Priory Farmhouse, reflecting the occupation of Finchden by Benedictines for ten years from 1868, before they moved to Canterbury. In fact, in the last century, Finchden was usually known as St Benedict's Priory or just The Priory.

From 1935 until the early 1970s, George Lyward ran a community for young people at Finchden Manor. After working with sixth form pupils in public schools who suffered from emotional problems, he realised he had a certain gift for helping such young people and set up Finchden at the request of a number of eminent psychiatrists. It was a unique community in the UK. Until his death in 1973, he devoted all his time and energy to running the centre and helped many young people. He was awarded the OBE for his work. The story is told in a book *Mr Lyward's Answer* by Michael Burn.

His son, Mr John Lyward, took over on his father's death but soon faced financial problems and difficulties in meeting fire regulations. The community had to close the following year. At the time he said: "There are 22 young people at the manor whose ages range from 15 upwards and eight staff. There is no maximum age limit and, contrary to local belief, few parents pay fees. In most cases, social service departments in the areas from which the boys come from pay the fees." He disliked calling the manor a 'school', and said he found it very difficult to describe what Finchden Manor was.

Today, Finchden has been divided up into several properties but the farm opposite is still called Priory Farm.

Houses in picturesque Bells Lane still bear the names Theatre Square, Theatre Cottage and Playwright Cottage, indicating that this lovely little street with it cascades of flowers was once home to Tenterden Theatre. Built in 1799, it stood on the east side of Bells Lane and was run by the Jonas and Penley Company which also had theatres in Folkestone and Lydd. An Act of 1788 lifted restrictions on theatres outside

London and allowed local magistrates to license them to operate a maximum of 60 days per year. The playbill advertising 'Peasant Boy' and 'Darkness Visible' is typical of those of the time that advertised the attractions for a single evening, listing the main play, the afterpiece, the songs and dance interludes, together with the cast and players. The theatre had closed by the 1840s. The home-made go-carts on which the boys are racing in the old picture might not be so popular now in this sought-after part of the town.

GATESDENE, OAKS ROAD

"Gatesdene", Tenterden.

This fine old house, pulled down in 2004, became a girls' school during the First World War, when Cliff House School moved from Thanet. Known later as Gatesdene School, it had a frontage along Oaks Road as well as Elmfield and took over the neighbouring property Playden before it closed in the 1930s. It was run by two sisters, the Misses Ellen and Fanny Bowers assisted by Miss R.F. Crump as house mistress. The original house was used mainly for music, dancing, meals and dormitories whilst Playden was used for classrooms. In due course Miss Ellen Bowers became the sole principal. A preparatory class for boys was started as well as school companies for Girl Guides and Brownies.

The academic side of the school was described in Thomson's Almanac: "The work follows from the syllabuses set for Oxford and Cambridge local examinations. Pupils are prepared for the examinations of the Associated Board of the Royal Academy of Music and Royal College of Music, the Royal Drawing Society and the London Institute for the Advancement of Plain Needlework. All games and open-air pursuits encouraged and PT is a prominent feature of school life. Great attention given to the general health and happiness of pupils. A limited number of day pupils taken."

After the school closed, Gatesdene became a guest house and then a private residence. The luxurious flats, now known as Elmfield Place, which replaced it are unusual in that the ground floor apartments have their kitchens below ground level with a spiral staircase.

CROWN INN, ST. MICHAELS

The Crown Inn, in the centre of St. Michaels, was probably built in the 1820s. The picture shows that the Inn belonged to Ashford Breweries before being taken over by Style and Winch in the early years of the 20th century. By the gate there is a little boy who is on foot and three other modes of transport are shown, an early car, a horse-drawn vehicle and a bicycle. The road to the left was not known as Grange Road until after the building of St. Michaels Grange further up the road by J.R. Diggle in 1897.

The actual building is little changed, although the climbing roses have gone as has the hedge and railings. The old Inn sign has been much improved with a magnificent crown and a sign advertises 'live sports'. The road junction has been altered to include a triangle to separate traffic and a wonderful hanging basket of flowers contrasts with the advertisements for goods from the nearby hardware store. Just visible against the dark background of a tree is the splendid St. Michaels village sign that was unveiled by Sir Donald Sinden, the actor, on Sunday 30 March 2008.

Embassy Cinema and Cellars

HIGH STREET, TENTERDEN   16188

The Embassy Cinema that replaced the Picture Theatre at East Cross opened in 1937 and closed in 1969. Its art nouveau facade is still imposing on the M&Co fashion store that replaced a supermarket. Next to the cinema was the Cellars Pub

and there was probably no other bar in England quite like it. It was below street level, was furnished with old casks, vats and barrels, and daylight could barely pierce the tiny windows. The whole of the ceiling had old bill cards, letters and mementoes hanging from it. The Cellars was closed in 1986 and is now a coffee shop.

The Stage Waggon, teamed by six or eight horses, was a common means of transport in the 18th and early 19th centuries. It was used for the transport of goods and for poorer passengers unable to afford the Stage Coach. Mr Hammond's Stage

Waggon left Tenterden every Monday morning and arrived at The George Inn, Borough, (where Mr Pickwick met Sam Weller in Dickens' novel) on the Wednesday morning. This was a fairly average journey which was probably extended somewhat if bad weather affected the condition of the roads. In 1807 Tenterden had two waggons (note the spelling with two gs) to London.

Modern buses that run from Tenterden still carry the name Stagecoach, but what a contrast in timing! This bus picking up passengers outside the Town Hall is en route to Ashford where they can board the Javelin high speed train that gets to St. Pancras in an astonishing 35 minutes: Total journey time little more than an hour.

Isemonger Toll House

The Isemonger Toll House stood on that stretch of the Rolvenden Road between Isemonger Farm and the junction with the Cranbrook Road. It was pulled down in November 1960 to widen the road. The Toll House was in the medieval borough of Castweazle, one of the six boroughs that constituted the Tenterden Hundred up to 1832 and persisted as census districts until 1871. The name Castweazle survives as it was given to the council houses on the Rolvenden Road built between the two World Wars.

A notice in *The Kentish Express* of 30 September 1874 offered for tender the Town Gate, Isemonger Gate and Cherry Gardens (Woodchurch Road) at £361 per annum. On 31 October 1874 the *South Eastern Advertiser* reported that a meeting of the Tenterden Turnpike Trust had leased them for £382 per annum for a period of 4 years.

Isemonger Farm still exists a little further down the road from the modern picture, but there is nothing left of the toll house and vehicles speed by unaware that in times past they would have had to stop to pay a toll.

THE WHITE LION

White Lion Hotel, Tenterden

The old coaching inn, The White Lion, has provided a place to eat, drink and, for some, to sleep in the High Street for at least 400 years, and probably longer. The present building is an 18th century, two-storey and attic building but it is quite likely that its history stretches back to the days of King Edward IV (1461-1483), whose badge was the White Lion. In the days when a town's charter was held directly from the King, inns often took the badge of the reigning monarch. The first written record shows that it was one of six licensed houses existing in Tenterden in 1577. The old picture, taken about 1900, shows a horse-drawn cart leaving the inn, the front of which is enclosed with hedges. Either side of the inn are private houses.

The garden has gone in favour of an open area for eating and drinking with large sunshades and the houses on the right have been replaced with what was the Midland Bank and is now HSBC. If you look closely you can see several detail changes to the building, the lantern over the front door has gone as have the window boxes.

SILVER HILL, ST. MICHAELS

Silver Hill, St. Michaels. Kent.

11.

Silver Hill, just on the St. Michaels side of the main entrance to Homewood School in the Ashford Road, was one of relatively few areas in Tenterden to suffer bomb damage in World War Two. In August 1944, a Doodlebug (V1 Flying Bomb) fell at the end of Ingleden Park Road causing damage to the teashop and surrounding buildings. These were later demolished to make room for 5, 6 and 7 Silver Hill but Ivy Cottage (weather-boarded house No. 8) and Cottenden (brick house No. 9) remain.

The name Silver Hill may simply relate to a number of silver birch trees which could have been growing there in earlier years. The scene now is barely recognisable as the same spot. This is now a very busy stretch of the A28 carrying many school buses and traffic to St. Michaels and Ashford.

SMALLHYTHE TOLL GATE

Small Hythe, Toll Gate.

Smallhythe, the former home of Ellen Terry, is now owned by the National Trust. Both of these pictures are taken near the river bridge just below Smallhythe Place, looking up the hill towards Tenterden with Ellen Terry's house on the right and they show that the buildings have changed little in 100 years.

In 1932, the gates here were one of two sets left controlling access to the Isle of Oxney, the others at the Ferry Inn on the road between Stone and Appledore, being removed that year. The gates at Smallhythe were owned by Kent County Council and under a recently passed Act of Parliament, Tenterden Borough and Rural Councils asked for them to be removed by 1 April 1932. This did not occur and it was rumoured that the council was dragging its feet because it did

not want to lose the income. They eventually came down one afternoon in November 1932, when Mr F.W. Greig (Deputy County Surveyor) and his assistant removed the gates and immediately placed at each end of the bridge the then familiar red-spotted danger signals. The last paying traveller was Mr L.S. Watson, an insurance inspector from Tunbridge Wells, who paid 6d (2.5p) at 2.29pm. He expressed great pleasure at the gates being removed and estimated that he must have paid at least a thousand sixpences over the previous few years. Mr Greig then drove the first free car over the bridge.

The bicycle in the old picture looks to have been a real bone shaker and in 1910 people might have been taken aback by the 2012 sign advertising a Music and Beer Festival.

Bowls, 1911

Tenterden Bowls Club was founded in 1908 with a four rink Green behind the White Lion Hotel. The early part of the club's history has been lost in the mists of time. In 1964 a new six rink Green was opened in Recreation Ground Road and the Club still plays there. About this time a Ladies' section was formed and from about 1985 matches have been played with mixed teams of ladies and gentlemen.

Tenterden Bowls Club, early 1970s

*Tenterden's mayor launches the first
wood at the Bowls Club, 2008*

Over the years the Club has had successes in the Weald of Kent Bowls League. One or two highlights of the last few years have been winning the Cinque Ports Mayor's Trophy in 1988, and successfully hosting the same tournament in 1999 and winning the Premier Division of the Weald of Kent Bowls League in 2004. Over the past 20 years with much hard work, generous donations and loans from members and other sources, the club has installed an automatic watering system and built toilets and a new clubhouse. The present clubhouse has photographs of the old thatched pavilion and the replacement pavilion that was opened in April 1932. The site of the original green is now a car park for the White Lion hotel.

GOLDEN SQUARE

Golden Square Tenterden

Golden Square is that part of Tenterden between the end of Oaks Road and the start of Woodchurch Road after crossing Beacon Oak Road. How it acquired the name Golden Square is a mystery. The area was known as New Town when it was first developed between the latter part of the 19th century and the beginning of the 20th century as housing began to be built away from the High Street.

In its day the little property on the left has been a fish and chip shop and a gentlemen's hairdresser, although it is now part of a house with the pavement outside protected from traffic by bollards where the road narrows. The trees that have grown to maturity now obscure the distant view of the church, but the buildings are little changed and a painter is busy up a ladder applying yet another coat of white to one of the cottages. There are signposts to the St. John Ambulance hut and to a public footpath.

KENT & EAST SUSSEX RAILWAY

Tenterden Station.

Work is currently underway to extend the restored Kent & East Sussex Railway from Bodiam to Robertsbridge, where it will meet up with the national rail network just as it did when the line to Tenterden first opened in 1900. That line, known as the Rother Valley Railway was the first line to be built under an 1896 Light Railways Act designed to provide services for those towns which had missed out during the Victorian boom times. Such lines were constructed as cheaply as possible, following the contours of the countryside rather than going through expensive features such as cuttings and tunnels. The Rother Valley line ran from Robertsbridge on the South Eastern & Chatham Railway between London and Hastings and there were stations at Bodiam, Northiam and Wittersham Road on the way to a terminus about a mile from Tenterden on the Rolvenden Road. Despite its position, the terminus was called Tenterden Station.

In 1903 the line was extended closer to Tenterden town centre. A new terminus, shown in our old photograph, was built at the end of Brewhouse Lane (so named because of the brewery at the rear of the Vine Inn) and called Tenterden Town Station. The road was renamed Station Road. The original terminus near Ashbourne Mill was renamed Rolvenden Station.

The name was changed to the Kent & East Sussex Railway and a new section of track, some eight miles, was laid to Headcorn, where it had its own platform adjacent to the Up side of the South Eastern & Chatham Railway from London to Ashford and Dover. Other stopping points were provided at St. Michaels Halt, High Halden Road, Biddenden and Frittenden Road.

After the Second World War, the Kent & East Sussex Railway remained a private company for a few years, but with rail nationalisation in 1948, it became a part of the British Railways network. The line closed to passenger traffic in January 1954 and the Tenterden-Headcorn section was taken up. The Tenterden-Robertsbridge section remained open for freight trains and seasonal hop picker specials to Bodiam until 1961 when the line was completely closed.

Despite official opposition, a small society was formed and was able to get a part of the line reopened and to work a limited number of trains. The line between Tenterden and Rolvenden was officially opened again in 1974, reaching Bodiam and its famous castle in 2000. Today it is a major tourist attraction in south-east England and has restored and runs a number of period steam and diesel locomotives and associated coaches. At Tenterden Town Station there is a museum, shop, buffet and a children's playground. Special events are organised including the ever popular Thomas the Tank Engine™ weekends, when an engine is adorned with the well-known face and the station staff dress up in character, including the Fat Controller.

Jireh Chapel, St. Michaels

The Jireh Chapel was built in 1869 for a Strict and Particular Baptist congregation which had previously met in the grounds of Homewood House and later in St. Michaels. The word Jireh means "The Lord will provide". The building was a typical Kent white weather-boarded structure which was re-clad in cedar in the 1960s. Reuben Weeks was Pastor from 1884 until 1922 and during his time there were many changes including the commencement of a Sunday school.

The chapel is still in use with services and prayer meetings four times each Sunday and on Wednesdays. The Sabbath School also meets on Sundays. The current Pastor is Gilbert W. Hyde. Although the trees and shrubs have grown and the old lamp post has gone, the building and the railings are much the same although much brighter and more welcoming.

HOP PICKING

Hop-picking in Kent

Until about 50 years ago, before the arrival of hop machines, the communities around Tenterden were expanded by the annual September invasion of happy-go-lucky hop-pickers from the East End of London, joining the locals in bringing home the harvest and often treating the occasion as their annual holiday.

Londoners made use of the Kent and East Sussex Railway to come to Tenterden at the weekends to spend their money in the shops and local hostelries and an annual open-air church service for hoppers was held at Smallhythe.

Tenterden had its fair share of hop gardens, and although there are still a few they are difficult to find today. Evidence of the industry remains in the oast houses that can be seen in most villages. At various times, British agriculture has gone through bad times and hop growing has been no exception. In the early part of the 20th century, there was much discontent amongst the farming community over the import of cheap foreign hops which led to demonstrations.

While most oast houses have been converted into lovely homes, some are also used as offices and the picture of two square oasts taken on the Smallhythe Road just outside Tenterden shows a complex of houses and businesses. Note the Kent horses on the cowls. Some oast houses were square as they were easier to build, but some farmers were of the opinion that a round design helped the hops dry more evenly.

Sheep and Cattle Fairs

For hundreds of years, sheep and cattle fairs were held annually in Tenterden High Street, one on the first Monday in May and the other on the first Friday in September. The animals were allowed to graze on the grass which was not mown and the stench and mess at the time these pictures were taken around 1890 must have been terrible. There were no sanitary arrangements in this part of town.

Many of the houses, including Borough Place in the background of the inset picture, were already there in the 17th century or earlier; and were built in the then revolutionary modern manner, around a central stack. There is still a 16th

century chimney stack at the eastern end of Borough Place, a building which was extensively altered in the 18th century when it became the Tenterden Workhouse. William Bright, a draper, bought the Workhouse from the Guardians in 1850 and converted it into the present six cottages.

The small house on the extreme left is Pittlesden Gate House which was at one time the home of Harry Swift, a bill poster (one can see bills outside on a large board). With his bucket and pasting mop on the end of a long pole, he was a familiar figure in the first half of the last century pedalling his bicycle in Tenterden and the surrounds, pasting bills for auctioneers, etc. Pittlesden Gate House still retains much of its 15th century external appearance.

After many protests about the mess caused by the fairs, the Tenterden Corporation purchased the present Recreation Ground in 1894 from the Dean and Chapter of Canterbury. So, twice a year this new venue for the fairs became quite a mess. For Tenterden Football Club that played there until the mid-1960s, it was essential to finish the season before the first Monday in May and not start playing again too early in September. One hoped it would rain to wash the mess away before play commenced! Fairs continued well into the second half of the 20th century before local farmers started taking their animals to the weekly markets at Rye, Maidstone and Ashford, which is now the only one for miles around.

The most noticeable change in this scene is, of course, the modern road surface with its kerbs, lamp posts and the full-grown trees. But the sharp-eyed will also have spotted that the war memorial is missing from the old picture. It was not erected until May 1920.

Tenterden Parish Church

There was probably a church on the site of St. Mildred's as early as 800AD but the earliest records of the present church are dated 1180 when the nave and chancel were built. The south and north aisles and the porch were added in subsequent centuries. The impressive tower, which is made of Bethersden marble, was built in the 15th century when Tenterden prospered due to the wool trade. In 1588, the tower was a beacon to warn the surrounding countryside of the approaching Spanish Armada. A feature of the church is the sundial over the porch. The old picture shows the

Rev. S.C. Lepard (vicar 1884-1906). The Rev. Philip Ward (vicar 1830-59) is one of the better known vicars having been married to Horatia, the illegitimate daughter of Admiral Lord Horatio Nelson and Lady Hamilton. Another popular vicar was the Rev. John Babington (1907-24), a widower, but his daughter Margaret who lived with him was even more popular as she was a tireless worker for the town and when they moved to Canterbury became a well-known figure for her work for the Cathedral.

The church has dominated the skyline of the town for centuries and the exterior has not changed much for the last 400 years, but the interior has altered to reflect trends with an electronic sound system and glass doors recently added to the porch.

Despite all the changes shown in this book Tenterden remains a delightful and traditional Wealden town and long may it continue to do so.